Praise for the Poetry of S

"Vikram's wordsmithing is outstanding. I have read much poetry and have never seen such creativeness as that of this author. She allows her words to flow with rhythm and deepness. The wisdom that comes through her is beyond any I've seen."
—Irene Watson, *Reader Views*

"In *Kaleidoscope: An Asian Journey of Colors*, Sweta Srivastava Vikram re-appropriates color. Cultures and mythologies collide along the way, and the result is a chapbook that feels like a quest. In the end, the colors are a map to identity. The child's pink tonsils or the bride's red sari are not symbols, but rather mile markers. Like Vikram's poems, they lead toward understanding."
—Erica Wright, Senior Poetry Editor, *Guernica*

"This slim chapbook is a quick bite. Poems appear and disappear in the blink of an eye, but linger in consciousness longer than you might think they would. The use of colors is fascinating to the desi mind; we, as one poem remarks, 'exist in a hue of experiences.'"
—Vidya Pradhan, Editor, *India Currents*

"This chapbook is the dazzling display of a poet who teases us with fresh imagery and delicate linguistic craftsmanship. The real joy of this collection is its potential to be read in a single sitting, multiple times, with each subsequent reading revealing new insights. For poetry virgins, this text demands no sophisticated knowledge of poetics and literary discourse. To put simply, it is an accessible piece of enjoyable writing."
—Orchid Tierney, Editor, *Rem Magazine*, New Zealand

"I dove into this book of poems quickly and eagerly, then slowed down to savor the words and the images, marveling over Sweta Srivastava Vikram's unique mix of grace, humor, and eloquence, which forms a medley of beauty and color."
—Susan Ortlieb, *Suko's Notebook*

"Sweta has woven such a spell with her word usage and the symbolisms that the most complex becomes the simplest of all."
—Smita Singh, *VAANI*, UK

"I'm glad I found a new South Asian author, and will be following Vikram's work closely in the future."
—Swapna Krishna

"Sweta Srivastava Vikram's *Because All Is Not Lost: Verse On Grief* shares her personal loss and, in return, comforts the reader. Her beautifully crafted poems take the reader on a voyage that has to be undertaken by each of us individually."
—Patricia Carragon, *Brownstone Poets*

"....there is a bit of defiance in her words as the color beige takes over in old age and she fights to remain red, youthful. Overall, *Kaleidoscope: An Asian Journey of Colors* is an even stronger chapbook poetry collection than Because All Is Not Lost because it deals more than with just emotion and healing. Sweta Srivastava Vikram is a gifted poet..."
—Serena, *Savvy Verse and Wit*

"This is a collection populated by a recognizable but richly diverse and dramatic cast of family characters."
—Mary-Jane Newton, *Cha: An Asian Literary Journal*

"Sweta's poetic voice flows like water smoothing and shaping stones. With great skill she uncovers, sometimes tenderly and other times more forcefully, the shroud of fog surrounding the feminine archetype... she has created and nurtured a garden, a wordscape, in which trust and healing can flourish."
—Nick Purdon, author *The Road-shaped Heart*

"Sweta Srivastava Vikram holds her work close. Fold it one way, a poem of loss appears. Fold it yet again for a poem of longing. Her work is as structurally sound as the elements. It soars with anticipation. Vikram reveals lovely and powerful poems that will long linger."
—Doug Mathewson, Editor, *Blink-Ink*

WET SILENCE
Poems about Hindu widows

Sweta Srivastava Vikram

Foreword by Shaila Abdullah

From the World Voices Series

Modern History Press

From the World Voices Series
Distributed by Ingram Book Group, Bertram's Books (UK),
Hachette Livre (France).

Library of Congress Cataloging-in-Publication Data

Vikram, Sweta Srivastava, 1975-
 [Poems. Selections]
 Wet silence : poems about hindu widows / Sweta Srivastava
Vikram. -- First edition.
     pages ; cm. -- (World voices series)
 ISBN 978-1-61599-256-0 (softcover : acid-free paper) -- ISBN
978-1-61599-257-7 (hardcover : acid-free paper) -- ISBN 978-1-
61599-258-4 (ebook)
 I. Title.
 PS3622.I493A6 2015
 811'.6--dc23
                                        2014040975

Published by Modern History Press
www.ModernHistoryPress.com

an Imprint of Loving Healing Press
5145 Pontiac Trail
Ann Arbor, MI 48105
www.LHPress.com   info@LHPress.com

Tollfree USA/CAN: 888-761-6268
FAX: 734-663-6861

Also by Sweta Srivastava Vikram

Poetry
Because All Is Not Lost
Kaleidoscope: An Asian Journey of Colors
Whispering Woes of Ganges & Zambezi
Not All Birds Sing
Beyond the Scent of Sorrow
No Ocean Here

Fiction
Perfectly Untraditional

Nonfiction
Mouth full: *A collection of personal essays and poetry*

For Anudit, my husband—
for always being my biggest fan

"Never doubt that a small group of thoughtful, committed people can change the world. Indeed, it is the only thing that ever has."

~ Margaret Mead

Contents

Silence became my lover, that's why

Foreword

I must admit that I had no idea what I was in for when I was asked to provide a foreword for Sweta Vikram's *Wet Silence*. My reaction to the book was immediate. The poetry grabbed me by the core, lifted me to heights I had not imagined, dashed me down upon the rocks, and brought me back to reality with an unexpected fierceness.

The voice in *Wet Silence* is of a mature poet who has come into her own, her verses pulsating and throbbing with raw passion. I connected with her immediately. Sweta's words have the unique ability to both surprise and empower. They deliver irony and wit with a certain wryness that makes for delectable reading. *Wet Silence* will mock you, startle you, puzzle you, and then shock you into silence and introspection.

Wet Silence provides new territory for the reader's imagination to explore, leaving one to wonder what pain and suffering could invoke such powerful emotions. The pleasures and terrors of an ordinary life come alive on the pages as readers struggle for a moral compass on which to base their reactions and judgments. Sweta is a wordsmith—a true craftsman who needs to be applauded and widely recognized for her art.

Sweta's poetry deals with the many faces of widowhood in India. In many regions and cultures, as soon as a woman becomes a widow, she loses control of many things, including her right to remarry, eat certain foods, or wear colorful clothes. She is shamed into silence, her destiny sealed once she puts on her white sari, as if she somehow is to blame for bringing death to the family's doorstep.

Wet Silence is a startling account of Indian widows—some who loved their spouses with devotion and fidelity, others who lived in fear or loathing of their significant others. The Hindi words—*chaddar, tulsi, neem, holi, pallu*—sprinkled at various junctions add to the flavor of the poetic narrative and infuse metaphoric and sensory value to the verses.

In Sweta's poems, we meet women who loved their husbands fiercely, yet did not want to be defined by the loss of their partners.

> *I am burning with desire.*
> *But all I see:*
> *my desires burning*
> *on the pyre along with your body.*

We also are introduced to women trapped in loveless marriages who tolerate their husbands' infidelity and don't have the will or right to speak out until the deaths of their spouses infuse them with courage.

> *Here I am, called a crude metaphor*
> *for not wanting to wake up under fouled sheets.*
> *Here I am, called inauspicious*
> *for being a widow on Holi and embracing colors of your*
> *love.*

Not wanting the stigma of being divorcées, many of these women stay in their unhappy marriages until the deaths of their partners set them free, only to be trapped once more by the white shroud of widowhood. For these women, there is no escape; their destiny is sealed.

> *I breathe broken air,*
> *even though his feet are still.*
> *Maybe this poem will free me*
> *from fifty years of life in prison.*

Only a few times in life will you read poetry that transports you to another world and shakes your very being. Readers, you have been forewarned: When you pick up this book, be prepared to plunge to unfathomable depths and soar to impossible heights. *Wet Silence* by Sweta Vikram will do that to you.

Shaila Abdullah, author,
Saffron Dreams and *Beyond the Cayenne Wall*

Acknowledgments

Wet Silence would still be a dream had it not been for the contribution, faith, and support of many people.

I'd like to express my gratitude to the widows and the female relatives of widows who confided their life stories in me and agreed to talk about a tabooed topic. It couldn't have been easy airing your familial secrets with a stranger or sharing your vulnerabilities. I admire your courage and am humbled by your faith in me.

I would like to thank Justen Ahren, West Tisbury poet laureate and founder of Noepe Center for Literary Arts, for his hospitality and support. It was at his residency that I wrote the first draft of this book. Special thanks to my fellow poets and writers, especially Ellen Goldstein, Milla van der Have, Sarah Levine, Joyce Yarrow, and Leah Zibulsky at Noepe Center for Literary Arts on Martha's Vineyard for their encouragement. I'd also like to acknowledge Anora McGaha and Barbara Bos of *Women Writers* for giving one of the first poems from *Wet Silence* a home in their magazine. Many thanks to my quiet and productive haven in NYC: The Writers Room. I am grateful to Nancy Agabian, Emily Berry, Linda Ganjian, and Zahida Pirani for co-creating a space and community that help me become a better poet and person. Adriana Cloud, I so appreciate what you do with your magical pen of proofreading.

To the stories and photographs that have inspired me along the way to bring a unique flavor to the poems in this collection, thank you.

To Dr. Jyotika Agochiya and the many people (psychologists and employees of women's organizations) who would rather go unnamed, many thanks for helping me understand the physical, behavioral, and emotional changes in women of different ages and how those changes could impact their desires and needs.

I am grateful for my family's encouragement and the support of my friends. Rashi Singhvi Baid, Nirav Patel, and Jaya Sharan: the book and I owe you so much. Thanks to my husband, Anudit, for always being there, encouraging me to listen to my heart, giving me the space that my artistic endeavors require, and for understanding why these books are important to me.

My immense gratitude to my editor, Sherry Quan Lee, for her astuteness and vision. Doug West, thank you for designing a book cover that is so wonderfully representative of what the book is about. And finally, I thank Victor R. Volkman at Modern History Press for believing in me and taking risks.

Introduction

The poems in *Wet Silence* are inspired by real life occurrences amongst educated, well-to-do, urban families in India. Many of the poems in the collection address the heavy hand of patriarchy still ruling one of the largest democracies.

The documents and research material available out there bring to light mostly what happens to many Hindu widows from a social viewpoint: when they are sent away or deprived of materialism and family property after they lose their husband or called inauspicious and ostracized. *Wet Silence* aims to target a bigger problem from an emotional standpoint: it brings to light the lack of dignity, sensuality and companionship in the life of Hindu widows. I interviewed a gynecologist to understand how desires and needs in women get affected with age... if at all.

Widowhood can take away respect from these women. Hindu men are quickly remarried but that's not common against women (Boomers and Generation X, that is). Many women spend their remaining days in the company of solitude, hanging on to memories.

While in many families (sons, traditionally) take care of their widowed mothers, the woman is expected to wear white, give up meat, and mourn her dead husband. These women are expected to consider themselves fortunate if their son and daughter-in-law care for them in their old age.

In the modern families, while the restrictions might be fewer but something things remain unchanged: the absence of a partner in the lives of most of the widows. It's one thing if the widowed woman chooses to not seek companionship; more often than not, society and their family make the choice for them.

Many widows were in healthy marriages and might miss their spouses. Equal number had arranged marriages and lived with domineering husbands and cruel in-laws. They had no choice but to put up with misogyny and sexism. Some of the women were two decades younger than their deceased husbands. The dead husbands sometimes had affairs with maidservants and beat up their wives. They kept mistresses. Sometimes, they cheated on the wife with her sister or abandoned the wife for a younger woman. Despite all that, a widow is expected to mourn her dead husband irrespective of what their marriage represented or how she was treated when the man was alive. She is expected to lead a life of celibacy and feel gratitude towards whoever showers any kindness.

My humble efforts are to highlight all of these various, untouched aspects of widowhood.

Wet Silence chronicles palpable stories of Hindu widows in India. The poems, inspired by true stories and personal interviews, bear testimony and reveal the harsh realities of widowhood from a never-before discussed angle.

I can hear a white cotton sari
weaving at the shop

My husband is leaving

Widowhood is trapping me unwillingly.

I can hear a white cotton sari weaving at the shop,
demonic voices sharp as the mustard paste in fish curry
speaking in whispers around the hospital corridor,
accusing me of standing and watching
his rotting flesh and dull eyes,
not brooding like soot on windows.

My husband is leaving.

It's his touch gentle as velvet,
his angelic tone that I'm seeking.
Bidding farewell to our dream,
my curse: I keep on living.

Craving you

In my eyes, a rainstorm gathers,
I write you a poem.
Your body burning on the pyre
lights a fire in my pen.

Your kiss reached
my lungs, I lost my heart.
Your touch burned
my words in the Indian summer.

How can I fill
the vacuum in my life
with anything else?

I press my fingers
against your memory—
the curse of being a poet,
feeling everything so deeply.

I miss you
for years after you are gone.

4

Spectator

I would like to mourn you for 24 hours
before the knives of tradition
with tongues thick like that of an ox,
shave my head, shatter my glass bangles,
snatch away colors and memories
and everything falls through my hands.

Waters swell in the Ganges.
The river doesn't rest
dusk beseeches us.
I want time
to name your bones.
Your slender mouth
I want to kiss for one last time
along with the dirt under your fingernails.
I am a spectator
as others wash your naked body with *Ganga Jal*
for one last time
and drape my trembling torso
in a white cotton sari.

I hate that the hand upon your chest isn't mine.
I hate that the hand wiping my tears aren't yours.

Ed Note: please see the Glossary on p. 51 for an explanation of common Hindi phrases used in this book

Note from a dutiful widow

I have made morning tea
for your spinster aunt
with vulgar imagination about the milkman.

I have dropped off
your brother at school for the past year
so he doesn't become a stranger in the dark.

I have taught dancing
to your teenage sister so she doesn't hide
a random man's face between her thighs.

I have served dinner
to your father, although he ignores his family,
obsesses about his neatly arranged love affair.

I have crocheted shawls
for your mother, filled holes
in her worn out dreams and family picture.

I'm exhausted from being alone in company,
my longing for you hasn't ceased.
Solitude is my partner in bed.

Weeping

In the dark garage
I accept there will be no more
sticks for the fire.

Winter blankets my longing arms,
whispers he is never coming.

I am not writing this poem
so the world can empathize;

why sacrifice my plea
for people who lay your naked body
on pyre, burn my wishes
as if I was toxic waste?

Weeping doesn't rescue a widow.

Never abandoned

Showers of rice and turmeric drowned us
as we walked around *Agni*,
completing our marriage vows.
Truth was hidden
underneath the garlands we had exchanged.

The countless times aunties
said you would never touch
my ebony skin, I felt like abandoned dust.
Bleach whitened the dark spots
of my family. Your name was tattooed
on my wrist to prove my love
was stronger than the ruins of Egypt.
My fingers were massaged with *Bhut Jolokia*,
so I could keep up the magic in the kitchen.
You weren't going to want
to taste me like nectar, my skin was lethal
like ghost chillies. Well, that was the assumption.

How do I tell anyone what you gave me?
Even when you had less hair and few breaths,
you kissed my questions,
we came crashing like a wave.
We contained each other.

Even the rain can't erase
the warm memories of our togetherness
the cold bones others try to break.

Ghazal

Dear husband: try to leave your scent behind.

Eyes follow me around,
asking me to wash
my muddy toes dirtied by the rain.
They say red
doesn't belong in my hair.
The voices of your children
I recognize as they call me names.
I sing in silence.
I wonder
if my shadow will be mine
after you are gone.

Dear husband: try to leave your scent behind.

I know
your *Old Spice* on my pillowcase
will drive me insane.
The music made
with our morning laughter
will forever haunt
my ghazals.
My tongue will burn
from wanting to kiss
the *Old Monk* breath
and words of love on your dark lips.

Dear husband: try to leave your scent behind.

Setting sun

Like a sack of rice in the pantry,
I am sitting quietly.
Bones are stiff and aching,
memory is slightly fading.

But I remember when you rolled and pressed
your ear to my cheeks in the mornings,

and when my feet were tired,
you would carry me in your arms,
gently place me on the rocking chair,
suck my toes, and caress my legs under my sari.

How we passionately took each breath,
wrapped between cotton sheets, for granted.
We didn't know.

Our blood

This poem is about our only son
who leaves me restless.
I die each day
looking at him.
He wants me gone.

Where did we go wrong?
I cradled his face with extra kisses,
the ones he missed getting from you.
I hugged him every day when he was little,
shared the plans you had made for his future.
He calls your memories a burden.

I sold my bones
as I worked three jobs
so he could become an engineer.
I wore white and lived as your widow
so he didn't have to share
me with another man.
My limbs seem useless to him today.

I cross my legs
but don't say a word—
there is not enough toothpaste in this house
to scrub out the foul taste of my hurt.

Silence sides with my grieving heart.

Holi

An excuse to touch—
flailing bodies burst with a series of fantasies.
Old men with potbellies and baldheads full of stolen poems,
middle-aged women slurring
over *bhang thandai* and old, Bollywood music.

Flesh yearns to converse with flesh on display,
eyes moan, confess hunger for an empty room with no ties.

Risqué hip signals on display
pores glisten with sweat on mahogany skin.

A rascal hand slithers over a stranger's belly,
carnal music whispered to breasts of unfamiliar women.
Handful of colorful powder and paint unleash the darkness
of unexamined life, desire to wake up in an unknown bed.

Each of the men and women present turn into something
I don't want to recognize.

People willing to walk on hot coal
to prove their chastity and test their lover's loyalty,
so easily flap their tongues where it doesn't belong
and present it as a synopsis for the festival of *Holi*.

Here I am, called a prude
for too much consciousness.

Here I am, called a crude metaphor
for not wanting to wake up under fouled sheets.

Here I am, called inauspicious
for being a widow on Holi and embracing colors of your love.

Without You

I don't want to sleep
without you looking at me.
I'm learning to do without
your arms soothing my nights.
I run my hands over your contours in my mind.
I didn't ask for this silence.

Black mask

My teeth have dropped,
my skin is burnt.
I don't exist.
You don't know
how my eyes
have become dark from dried up sorrow.
I stretch my senses,
no one sees my vision.
Without you, everything that pleased me
tastes bitter like gourd.
Rotis and condolences don't nourish me.
If you ask me
what's gone wrong,
I don't want to tell you.
There are so many unpleasant things
I want to forget.
Silent and starving,
I prowl through memories of our sweet days
when I wasn't forced to wear a black mask.

Nectar

At family gatherings, you would try to steal
a kiss, wrap me in your arms,
run your hands underneath my *pallu*.
When I would say a no
with my kohl-drenched eyes and silent smile,
you would pout your stiff lips,
chant a new song to the stars.
I would squeeze nectar from my breasts,
pour a few drops into your cup of tea.
With lover's hesitation,
I would hint,
you know which cup is yours.
Your stiff throat, ridged tongue,
and smell of fresh sweat were a sign:
you approved of the juicy secrets of my ebony hands.
Our tongues would entwine,
but our kisses didn't touch,
such was our passion.

You are gone.
Lone nights keep me company
as my breasts sag to waistline.
This is my torture—
silent walks on the terrace,
seeking your scent in the summer breeze.
My days are dying
along with my smile.
My *pallu* is damp
from my tears.

The rustle in mango leaves

I look for hidden meanings
in every folded sari,
in the crease of your shirts.
The extra hot mango pickle
that won't stiffen
your smile and indignant tongue.

I pull out your fragrance
from my memories,
find a quiet spot under the mango tree.
The same place where
we laced ourselves last summer,
when your arms made me
feel secure on moonless nights.

With you gone, I'm the rustle
in mango leaves,
solitude is my partner.

Nickname

You wore a *Tulsi* thread
around your thin neck,
I put jasmine oil on my wrist.
You draped my tiny shoulders
with a silk sari you bought
from your last trip to Chennai.

We secretly met
between the ocean and the rocks—
a point where all lovers gave out their secrets.
We knew all their nicknames,
just not the one the universe had picked out for us—
I remember the caution
in the evening air
but I was busy overhearing what was never mine.

You promised
we'd grow old together.
You would serve me
tea in bed in exchange
for gurgles and intimacy.
You would nibble my toes
for every time I gossiped.

What I wouldn't give
just to see you one more time.
Just to tell you some secrets.
To hold your face
in amorous delay,
to place my head
on your beating, weak chest.

Vulnerable

I am afraid to fall
asleep
because dreams don't promise
I will see his dead face
with my eyes closed.

**I didn't promise
to sleep in your shadow**

I water my memory of you

Matchsticks and mirror won't burn
the poems you wrote
while untangling my braid,
the secrets we whispered
to the curves of my hips,
the way wind cut
through our tender skin.

The names we recited
of our imaginary children.
The rooms we built
where sorrow would never find us.
You watched me spread
wet sheets on the clothing line,
pray to the sweet smell of *tulsi*.

At dawn, I sit like rust.
I water my memory of you—
it is all I have of you
along with your empty words
in the home we never built
where the mosquitoes feast on my skin.

Forbidden

I feel the loneliness of the ocean,
but I refuse to cry.
I didn't plant roses in your memory;
no need to water your grave.

Fragrance was forbidden in our marriage
unless it meant a younger woman's flesh.
The wind reminded me
of the stench every time you came home.

I wasn't a bird,
who flew over nests in search
of what it could claim to be its own,
when you were alive.
I didn't forbid you
to sleep with others
because you were never mine.

What does a servant girl know?

I was plucking chillies
when you stared at my lips—
said I needed no lipstick,
that nature had been kind to the contours.
You begged me for a taste
of the small, hot pepper.
You sucked my fiery tongue.

I believed you.
What does a servant girl know?

You drank from my breasts,
nicknamed them Serrano chillies.

I believed you.
What does a servant girl know?

You entered inside me,
but the room remained empty.
In many places, monsoon came early,
but the stains on my body remain unwashed.
I should have known.

I wished you would stay.
When you didn't,
I wrote you a letter.
We talked about
what you wanted to hear.
The streetlights went out,
for decades the pattern followed.

As your bones turn to ashes,
I ask why love had to be so blinding?
Why I couldn't crush the Serrano chillies,
apply a paste on your tongue
that had burnt me with lies?

Your wife

It was three mornings before *Diwali*
when I saw your children in Chandni Chowk.
I introduced myself to your wife;
she too was buying green glass bangles,
your favorite,
to embrace you and the New Year.

I wanted to ask so many questions—
what was she doing in the hot sun
in one of the oldest parts of New Delhi
when you had made sure
her feet were washed with rose petals every morning.

Are you trying to turn her into me?

Funny how festivals increase the gap
between your touch and my wanting hips,
she gets to taste the deep flavors
of *pakoras* and *masala chai* long after they burn
your lips, while I fast waiting
and hoping you will find your way back to me.

Other men notice your prints
on my breath;
you were everything to me.
But I remained a ghost story
in your life—
a fish bone that no one wants
in the throat long after the fish is dead.

Pretense

When I hear belts unbuckle,
I say your name to taste you.
The sound cuts
through my brown flesh,
I become wounded again.

But I admit our secret to no one.
I pretend we shared a love story
and named waves in the Arabian Sea
when I was only a shadow walking behind you.

Everybody falls
in their own eyes at some point in life.
I did
when you slipped
like rain from my fingers
and uttered
Stupid woman, you are nothing
even on your death bed.

Hypocrisy

You wanted me full
of meat and bones,
but you kept
an eye on those
with thin skin and low self-esteem.
Perhaps, they were easier to break
than a strong woman like me.

I want to cut
the brown nipples you licked
when your bodies moaned in air.
I could smell
what I didn't see.

I see your hypocrisy.
I complain with light finger-strokes
on your thighs. I try to draw
an invisible boundary—
but I fail.

You might have died last month,
but I know when I stopped breathing.

Curry

You liked my skin smelling
of freshly roasted red chilli mixed with sea salt.

You kissed my braided hair,
the way you caressed the silhouette
hidden underneath the *pallu* of my sari.

You teased: the secret
to a good tasting marriage was the curry
the woman made in a hurry when her husband
dipped inside the sacred vessel. Our whispers
infected the kitchen, our bodies
fell and rose, spoke in voices only our lips heard.

But when warm blood trickled
between my legs three years in a row,
you called me and the empty bassinet tasteless.

I became the reason for your drinking.
I became the reason you found a new curry to catch.

The question

I want to follow *Yama*,
the lord of death,
and fight for your life
with my thin lips and blind eyes.

I would lick
your pain if I could.
I would swallow
your anguish like it was sugarcane juice.

Death doesn't frighten me.

Yama doesn't listen to me.
He says, *ask your husband*
if he will mourn for you
if I, death, take you instead of him?

I know the answer to my question.

Sour milk

There is no woman who goes to bed
and doesn't dream
but when you asked
if you could invite your old lovers in our lives,
the vermillion in my hair
was replaced with chilli powder,
the scent of rose behind my ears
smelled like burnt pepper.

I was a good-natured woman.
I wondered if you liked strawberries.
I ate after feeding you.
I kissed your freckles and heavy lids.

But you called me a *whore*,
kicked me with shoes covered in mud
threw cusses dipped in bitter oil
because I wouldn't share our bed.

I sit by the window, away
from your shadow
and write about broken love,
no longer dreaming.

My sister's husband

Sometimes I wanted to kiss your neck
when you came out
of the shower,
but even the fragrance of the soap
couldn't wash away the stench at home—
the hint of familiarity
mixed with pearls of betrayal I didn't recognize.
I was nineteen.
You were two decades older and my sister's husband.

At family dinners,
the smiles you would direct at me.
After family dinners,
the way you would spread
my trust along with hips.
The morning after family dinners—
you would remind me how to act
in bed when I wanted to snuggle
because you were my sister's husband.

You didn't tell me you had plans of your own—
you would always remain my sister's husband.

I sit on the kitchen stool
wondering how it'll all end.
I can't spend the rest of my life
rearranging striped cushions in your memory—
you were my sister's husband.

Misogynist

I want to gather threads
from the sky, join the stars
that light up the dead roses
he buried in his garden.
Show the world
his silly secrets,
his relationships with women,
the tip of his unused
cigar stuck between his front teeth.

If I'd been taught
how to curse,
I would have spelled out
his deserving name.
I'd call him something foul.
I know, I know.
Foul is dirty, fowl is a bird.
Yes, he was a dirty bird.

But I choose to become the woman
who knows the meaning of the veins
on her sociopathic dead husband's forehead,
and makes sure his memories aren't around forever.

I burn
stories about him along with his corpse.
This victory is mine, misogynist.

Broken

A line of betrayal ran
from the crease in his lips
to the line running between my breasts.

There was no one I could tell
A broken man is like a ghost—
he haunts when alive.

I smelled him in the maid's room,
in every chilli she chopped
to spice up what never was bland in our life.

There was no one I could tell
I can't cope any longer.
I am broken.
I will feel no tears when he is dead.

Hostage

There was nothing boring
in the rhythm of our things.
I pine for those days
when you loved me.

The way you crumpled my cotton sari,
held me from behind my waist.
I didn't loosen my grip
on your hair.
The fabric that had tied us together
became loose, when you decided
to walk out and sniff fresh meadows.

I didn't turn you into a pig,
as hearts cold as clay like to proclaim.
Pigs are loyal,
develop relationships with their mates,
remain family-oriented, I am told.
Pigs like *you* perform acts
that I won't mention in my poem.

**Silence became my lover,
that's why**

Silence became my lover

Your world was between my hips,
others whispered with *neem* on their tongues.
But we never thought of our passion that way.

We were suffering, sleeping
on questions that we didn't dare to ask.
Did our kisses become cancerous along with your lungs?

My tongue licked your earlobes,
looking for words—

sometimes there are no adjectives or adverbs
that work when there are unsaid words to be said.

Silence became my lover, that's why.

Just so you know, my every kiss was real.
I wrapped them in turmeric and sandalwood,
left them in your urn wrapped in a white sheet.

Heartbeat

Were you hiding
beneath the weight of your empty
promises when I thought I saw you
in the moonlight, behind the banyan tree?

With a broken candle,
I walk barefoot with anklets,
call out to you in my dark hours—
your heartbeat has answered before.

We had a simple life,
your heart promised to beat for me.
Your death changed everything.

Some promises dissolve in the rain,
emerge as poems.

Fifteen

When girls my age were trying out bangles,
my pores were opening up,
my feet were lighting fires—
your hands over my blouse,
you would lean into me.
That was a sign that a kiss was about to happen.
Your mouth against mine—
your breath scented with mint,
my teenage breasts washed with rose petals.

I didn't know
your every breath was miraculous.
That when I lifted your eyelids,
there was no story of our future in them.
A breathing heart was a given
like the wetness of June, I believed.

What did I know?
I was fifteen.
You are dead,
I am still trying to understand.

Solitude

When I try to open our bedroom door at midnight,
silence turns the key,
loneliness sleeps upon our pillow.

There is dust on our sheets,
where you once kissed my navel and thighs.

My chest swells like the ocean,
I hold in the waves.

Seeing ancient books of love poems
unopened on your desk,
I scream:

rain on me, universe,
cool the fire on my tongue.

I am afraid to fall asleep,
I am scared of the solitude
in my dreams.

Unshared words

I dreamt of you last night—
your cream *chaddar* tied into a knot
with my red *sari*, our hungry bodies making

rounds of Agni, uttering promises
we never talked about.
Did we know their meaning?

It was a weird dream.
In it, we looked happy.
But if that were the truth
I would have shown you
this letter when you were alive.

Eulogy

When we think
we can fix something,
there is no dearth of explanations.
But truth is truth—
like tasting a drop of ghost chilli infused tequila.
Even after twenty minutes, you can't feel the tip of your tongue.
Do details matter?
The *chai* was burnt.
The *daal* had more turmeric than the yellow in a sunflower.
The okra wasn't deeply fried, so your arteries are still alive.
The yolk in the egg decided to flood your toast.
You brought the blood-dried guns to our living room.
You found resolutions in cleavage that wasn't mine.
It wasn't the *chai*; the lies burnt your tongue.
You took the knife; cut me with your words.

Terrible accidents happen,
such is life.
They don't stir me,
or make my spirit drop.
You couldn't remain tied to a bed.

I am a lady,
but I didn't promise
to sleep in your shadow.

We kept our dirty laundry
on separate shelves in the same closet.

I'll rise

It wasn't bad enough,
I had to kiss an old man's mouth
with no smile or teeth. I never
leapt with delight in your embrace.
Now you know,
my salty tears didn't mean a sweet reaction.

I have been written off by your family.
To keep the money from leaving,
they roll dice, throw stones of selfishness.
Lies sit on their teeth
as they smile for society,
I throw up on the inside.

Your son reaches between my thighs
to find the treasure he's eyed from when you were alive.
I hold curses in my mouth,
naked bodies feel like dead twigs.

Your daughter creeps inside
my wedding collection, her mouth
swells up with curses on seeing my jewels.
I want to give up listening.

Your ex-wife with sugarcane sweetness
layered on her lying tongue, enquires if I liked
your sagging body rubbed against mine in the midst of summer.
I don't know, I say. *I haven't tasted worse.*

Your mother with short legs
bent from the waist bludgeons me
with *can you trust the sand,*
always moving—ready to submit to the ocean?

You never pulled yourself together for me.
But like the autumn breeze,
I'll indignantly rise, and sing songs of freedom.

You were always nothing

You stenciled your name on my thigh
like I was a used car in a mechanic's shop.
I swallowed the odor
of abandoned dust on the mantle
to keep the peace.
I scream only in my dreams.

Sure, I didn't cook a five-course meal.
My hair was tied up in a tight bun.
My silk saris were pleated
to pay our bills, put meals on the table.
When you were sick,
I gave you oxygen from my lungs.
We were childless,
you wanted my sister
to talk to me. Really?
You expected me to learn
the ten ways to lick your weathered skin.

I asked for an ounce
of respect, not even your love.
I had forgotten
you'd promised me nothing at all.

Why am I telling you all this?
You aren't listening.
Even dead,
you know how to break me down.

Secrets in my belly

There is fire in my belly
but no heat in my heart.
Hate to lose
anything—
be it memories, moments, bangles,
or my husband's breath.

Placing my bosom on your bare chest,
I knead your ribs with my ribs;
I hold your face between my breasts,
hope your swollen eye lids will open
and wink at me.

His breath is withdrawn
along with his magic.
I can't bring myself to accept
what all I've lost.

I don't keep secrets.

Passage of time

For an entire year, I watched
my bare arms and broken spirit
lift white cloth in the air,
drown washed sheets in the river.
I lost myself to the dark waters.

Will I be touched by another man,
wake up to bedraggled hair,
I wondered as I thrust
an index finger into my navel.

I miss
the inside jokes we shared.

I leave my windows unlocked.
It's June. The monsoons are here
to quench the parched earth,
but I still haven't invited anyone inside.

A widow's confession

My life is defined
between your corpse and your family's gaze.

I don't laugh at children with broken limbs.
I don't inhale the scent of roses.
I don't suck mangoes.
I don't smash crow skulls on the pavement.
I don't stalk lovers with rolling eyes.
I don't see your silhouette in the folds of my skin any longer.
I don't harbor illusions that my name was on your last breath.

But I can't hold my breath any longer—
my body is on fire.
I curse
the dirty rain
that leaves my white sari
clean.

You have been gone seven years;
I am still expected to be virtuous.

I don't want thumb approvals from your family.

Burning

My body doesn't own
fingerprints of strange men's hands.
No names. No fingers
running up and down my body.
I am burning with desire.
But all I see:
my desires burning
on the pyre along with your body.

Forewarned

A toothless astrologer had warned
my family: *your daughter*
will get trapped.

There will be no prints
of happiness on her front door:
the palmist with a shaved head and long ponytail had foretold.

No one understood truth
littered like watermelon seeds
pouring from the tarot card reader's mouth.

Maybe because no one tried
to listen from their heart.

I try to breathe
even though your feet are still.

Maybe this poem will free me
from fifty years of life in prison.

Wet silence

"I know it is a bad thing to break a promise, but I think now
that it is a worse thing to let a promise break you."
                    — Jennifer Donnelly, *A Northern Light*

You didn't love life.
Should I pity you?
You knew your mind was torn
like a widow's wedding dress.
Our children hid
behind the closet
knowing you'd be home soon.
No one wanted your attention.
They had seen rum handprints
on their mother's arms and face,
revealing their father's addiction.

To hide the secret,
I bit my tongue
and wore disappointment
on my shoulders, covered it with *dupatta*.

You dragged me by my throat,
I knew it wasn't the right way
for a husband to treat his wife.
As you became thicker,
the bed grumbled.
You took big bites of my bones,
sucked my marrow—
I noticed cobwebs on the ceiling,
waiting for you to pull out
another stream of unpunctuated slangs.
You left me feeling like a
freshly dug grave
as wet silence became my friend.

To hide the secret,
I bit my tongue
and wore disappointment
on my shoulders, covered it with *dupatta*.

I will not say, *"Drown me"*
because your ashes are still floating in the Ganges.
I will not allow
my marital promises to break me.

Working girl

Do happy people keep diaries?
I'm too old to be surprised
and you're too dead to give me an answer.
I can't go back to my hooded silence.

For a month, rent wasn't paid.
For a month, our daughter didn't hear
the rustling of homework sheets.
For a month, your mother
coughed crimson droplets in her *chai*.
For a month,
we stuffed emptiness and threats
in our stomachs.
For a month,
we sifted through your ashes, your memories.

I told you I wanted to read and write,
but you insisted my fingers belonged
in the spice rack to fetch you flavors.
You never asked where I wanted my hands,
I wish you'd paid attention.

I want to make sure
no one is hungry or hurt again,
many shadows enter my room at night.
My soul is tired
but my feet are resting
as I smile at my client list to hold my own.

Willpower

I am a woman
who can be left in a desert,
and I'll come back smelling of jasmine.

Glossary

Agni—a Hindu deity, one of the most important of the Vedic gods. He is the god of fire and the acceptor of sacrifices for onwards conveyance to other deities.

Bhang thandai—a cold drink prepared with a mixture of almonds, fennel seeds, watermelon kernel, rose petals, pepper, vetiver seeds, cardamom, saffron, milk, sugar, and cannabis plant. It is used as an intoxicant during *Holi*.

Bhoot Jolokia— also known as Ghost Pepper is the world's hottest pepper.

Chaddar—sheet

Daal—a sauce made from lentils and spices, usually served with rice.

Diwali—a Hindu festival of lights.

Dupatta—a length of material worn as a scarf or head covering, typically with a salwar, by women from South Asia.

Ganga Jal—sacred water from the River Ganges in India.

Holi—a Hindu spring festival celebrated in February or March in honor of Krishna.

Masala chai—is a distinctive style of milk-based tea.

Neem—a tropical Old World tree that yields mahogany-like timber, oil, medicinal products, and insecticide.

Pakoras—A deep-fried fritter made of vegetables in a chickpea batter, served as an appetizer or a snack in South Asian cuisine.

Pallu—the long trailing part of the saree that can be draped around and across the shoulders.

Rotis—an Indian Subcontinent, unleavened flat bread made from stone ground whole wheat.

Tulsi—or *Holy basil* is a sacred plant in Hindu belief.

Yama—In Hindu mythology, Lord Yama or Yamraj is referred to as the god of death.

About the Author

Sweta Srivastava Vikram, featured by *Asian Fusion* as "One of the most influential Asians of our time," is an award-winning writer, three times Pushcart Prize nominee, Amazon bestselling author of nine books, novelist, poet, essayist, and columnist who currently lives in New York City with her husband. Her work has appeared in several anthologies, literary journals, and online publications across nine countries in three continents. A graduate of Columbia University, Sweta reads her work, teaches creative writing workshops, and gives talks at universities and schools across the globe.

Visit the author's website at www.swetavikram.com

Brave New Collection
Honors Women's Spirit Worldwide

No Ocean Here bears moving accounts of women and girls in certain developing and under-developed countries. The book raises concern, and chronicles the socio-cultural conditions of women in parts of Asia, Africa, and the Middle East. The stories, either based on personal inter-views or inspired by true stories, are factual, visceral, haunting, and bold narratives, presented in the form of poems.

"Sweta Srivastava Vikram is no ordinary poet. The 44 poems in this slim volume carry the weight of unspeakable horrors and injustices against women. Sweta's words span the globe. Her spare and evocative phrases weave a dark tapestry of oppressive conventions that in the telling and in our reading and hearing, she helps to unravel."

—Kay Chernush, Founder/Director,
ArtWorks for Freedom

ISBN 978-1-61599-157-0
From Modern History Press
www.ModernHistoryPress.com

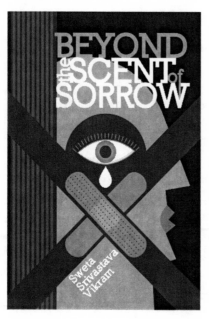

Beyond the Scent of Sorrow delves into the challenges faced by women on a global level. The eucalyptus trees in southwest Portugal are used as an archetype to symbolically elicit the challenges women face in today's world. Boldly, the poems which are lyrical, literal, short, and succinct, profess the unkind capabilities of mankind.

"Sweta's poetic voice flows like water smoothing and shaping stones. With great skill she uncovers, sometimes tenderly and other times more forcefully, the shroud of fog surrounding the feminine archetype... she has created and nurtured a garden, a wordscape, in which trust and healing can flourish."
—Nick Purdon, author of *The Road-shaped Heart*

"Sweta Srivastava Vikram holds her work close. Fold it one way, a poem of loss appears. Fold it yet again for a poem of longing. Her work is as structurally sound as the elements. It soars with anticipation. Vikram reveals lovely and powerful poems that will long linger."

—Doug Mathewson, Editor *Blink-Ink*

ISBN 978-1-61599-097-9
From Modern History Press
www.ModernHistoryPress.com

Introducing the World Voices Series

This series highlights the best English-language autobiography, fiction, and poetry of diverse voices from Africa, Asia, the Caribbean, and South America.

The Blue Fairy and other tales of transcendence
By Ernest Dempsey

Iraq Through a Bullet Hole: A Civilian Wikileaks
by Issam Jameel

The Road-Shaped Heart
by Nick Purdon

Beyond the Scent of Sorrow
By Sweta Srivastava Vikram

No Ocean Here
by Sweta Srivastava Vikram

A Short History of the Short Story
By Gulnaz Fatma

Ruskin Bond's World: Thematic Influences of Nature, Children, and Love in His Major Works
By Gulnaz Fatma

from Modern History Press
http://www.modernhistorypress.com/world-voices/

CPSIA information can be obtained at www.ICGtesting.com
Printed in the USA
LVOW07s0005240715

447456LV00002B/53/P